Joi

I hope you find
Comfort and validation
in this book.

♡

Nicole

Post-Partum
My Language

My true
account of the 4th
trimester

Post-Partum My Language
My true account of the 4th
trimester
Copyright © 2018 Nicole Kumi

All rights reserved. No part of
this book may be reproduced,
scanned, or distributed in any
printed or electronic form without
permission

Dedication

This book is dedicated to my daughter, Ava. Without you I never would have had this experience and opportunity to transform into the woman I am today. Without you I wouldn't be driven to make the changes that are necessary when it comes to maternal healthcare. Without you, this version of me wouldn't exist. May you recognize the power that comes with your presence baby girl, and understand how crucial your role has been since birth.

A Note from the Author

This book was comprised by a series of journal entries that I had written during my post-partum journey. This book began as a source of therapy for me and resulted in me shifting my life's passions to increased awareness and education for maternal mental health. I couldn't understand why I was having this experience and struggled to understand what I had done wrong. I recognized that I did everything right, and this was the path that was designed for me. I needed to walk through this darkness so that when I climbed out, I could use my journey to shed light on another woman's path. I am now choosing to do that in the work I do, and one day, my daughter will be mentally and emotionally prepared for motherhood and know that she and her mother contributed to that.

The Test

+ PREGNANT! Sheesh! What I saw on

that little test created such a range of emotions for

me that day. Pregnant huh? In that very moment

my brain raced all over the place and had me

seriously questioning what the hell I had gotten

myself into. Just like most women I had always

thought about having children, and dreaming

about what it would be like, but in that moment, I

wondered if I made a wise decision. Most people tell you the day they found out they were pregnant was magical, and a day they will never forget. I am not saying that I was not thrilled to have gotten pregnant, but suddenly, the thought of being responsible for some little life other than myself scared the living shit out of me. I stood there looking at the test and staring at myself in the mirror and realizing I did not recognize the girl staring back at me. I no longer was the 34-year-old married woman with "no kids." Somehow, in that very minute I saw myself as more mature and with the face of a mother. I was experiencing something very strange, out of the ordinary for me, and at that moment, I knew I was about to pass out. I vigorously threw water on my face all while dry heaving over the bathroom sink. "Get your shit together Nicole" is all that I could manage to mumble to myself through the mirror about 5o times over, yet I could not get my shit together, not then and certainly not later.I walked down the steps, and my husband was sitting at the kitchen table. My inner voice was telling me to breathe, and I could only imagine what he was thinking when he saw me awkwardly smile, stumble down the steps, and chug an entire glass of water. My husband is a kind, patient, understanding man who seems to remain calm in the worst of situations, so I knew I did not have anything to worry about. "Just tell him "My inner voice was saying, but I did everything except that. Sure, he looked at me waiting to hear me freak out about something that happened at work, or something else, but I never did, and he continued to walk on eggshells waiting for something to happen.

The rest of the evening was a blur as we had dinner, washed the dishes, talked about our days and so on. He literally could have told me he shot someone, and I would have said "Well isn't that nice." I knew he was thinking something was up, but again, the most patient and understanding man I know, he never pushed me. We sat on the couch and watched some tv and somewhere during Law and Order I started crying. "Ok, there it is, what is going on?" he asked me. At this point I am sobbing uncontrollably and unable to tell him anything. He moved closer and put his arm around me reassuring me that whatever was going on was time sensitive and it would pass. Boy was he ever so wrong. "Baby, I'm pregnant" I managed to get out between sobs. "I, I, just don't know if this is the right thing to do, and how are we going to do this, and are we really ready?" "Nicole, why are you crying? Didn't we try to get pregnant so that we could get pregnant and have a baby? I am really confused, and happy too." As calm as he is, my husband is very direct and clear, so he was having a hard time already understanding my uncertainty with this whole life event. "Yes. We did try and get pregnant so that we could have a baby, but it happened and now we are going to have a baby." I could tell he was still confused with the information and my erratic response to it, but he just held me tight, said he was happy and that we were going to be alright. Hmmmm alright? I don't know about you but finding out I was pregnant was the last time I ever felt "alright." The pregnancy brings about a host of feelings and emotions that a million people have written about to attempt to educate the pregnant women about. However, what really scared me to death was what was going to happen after this baby was born, that was if I went full term with this baby. In that instant, in my husband's embrace was the day my life forever changed, the anxiety began, and nothing would ever be the same.

The Pregnancy

Everyone has a different story about their pregnancy and how they felt and looked during this time. People would tell me that I would feel beautiful and confident in ways I never thought I could. Honestly, I never got that feeling of beauty and comfort. The feeling I experienced the most was confusion about what was happening to my body, and when would I finally look pregnant and not just like a busted can of biscuits people were talking about behind my back. I had worked hard to lose about 50lbs the year or so before for our wedding, and I was in the best shape of my life when I got pregnant, so watching my waistline expand "again" was not something I enjoyed or found to be "beautiful".

I worked out diligently for most of my pregnancy and a lot of people would say "where is that belly?" I laughed at those comments, and secretly smiled thinking "Wow, I must look really good." It was around week 30 when things started becoming difficult. Some of the maternity clothes I purchased at week 20 were no longer cute, or even fitting for the most part. I did not realize there were different stages of maternity ware, so imagine my surprise when I had to go back for round two. Nothing like a blow to your ego, and that beautiful pregnancy body I was still looking for. Week 30 is also where I started to trade in my high intensity workouts for more yoga focused routines and began to embrace yoga. I started moving slower around the house and chasing sleep at night due to hip pain and the inability to breathe the way I used to. The weeks went on and so did the weight. I found myself looking in the mirror saying, "what in the hell has happened to this body?" It appeared that I gained most of my pregnancy weight in the final 10 weeks (a whopping 60lbs total). I remembered friends of mine saying how much they gained and either thinking "that is nothing" or "holy shit that is a person". I did not think that I would fall into the latter category myself by week 40.

I never understood woman who rushed their pregnancies at the end or tried to dance and make labor happen non-organically. That was until I reached week 40 for myself. Dear God! There was not one thing I did not try to get this little bundle out of my uterus soon enough. I danced, I drove, I rolled on stability balls, I prayed, I squatted, and even thought about having wine. People would say "try having sex, it really works." Those people were never 40 weeks pregnant and 60lbs heavier because while sex may work, I was not working for it. Showering and getting dressed for work each day had me feeling like I was nothing shy of an Olympic athlete who deserved a medal. Going to work for a full day was like training for a marathon someone else signed me up for. Each day felt like it had 40 hours in it, and I was unable to sleep for 38 of them.

I was a person who valued my sleep in an insane way. I got to bed around 10am and made sure I got my full 8 hours of sleep each night. If I didn't get that, chances were I was going to be a bit moody at some point during the week, but at least I'll get my workouts in and that would balance things out. Now, I was not sleeping, not working out, and eating like a 14-year-old boy who couldn't gain weight if he tried. Life as I had known it was taking a very hard left down a road I had never traveled.

My due date was arriving this week and I had not even started to efface or any of that good stuff yet. My blood pressure was high, and I was sent in for observation the week before but sent home after it regulated. We decided to have an induction on her due date, since I was over being pregnant, and hoping to avoid her being born on her dad's birthday. One thing I learned, you cannot manipulate nature, because as uncooperative as my body was at the end of my pregnancy was nothing compared to how my induction didn't even work.

We were scheduled to head to the hospital on January 4, 2018, which was a Thursday and her due date. We had the car packed and were heading to The Outback to have our last supper when I received a phone call from the hospital telling me they had to cancel the induction as they have no rooms. Seriously!!!! At first, I was like "are you joking? Is this a joke"? The nurse explained to me because my induction was not a medical necessity I was being bumped until tomorrow in the event they have room for me. I hung up the phone and my husband pulled the car into a parking lot. He asked me what happened and through laughter and tears I told him all the while, feeling like I was being pranked. We texted family and friends to explain what happened and then had a big dinner. In that moment I thought about ordering a bottle of wine but figured that would be frowned upon, so I settled for a 9oz filet and a brownie sundae. That night I laid in bed wondering if tomorrow the day would be or if I would be sitting around eating brownies when they called with the same ordeal. Whatever happened I was just looking forward to meeting my little girl in the next few days.

The Induction

Friday came and we arrived at the hospital all prepared for the induction to begin that evening, and hopefully meet baby girl on Saturday. Let me tell you it was the coldest weekend in January so far, and honestly ever in my life. I was 60lbs heavier and freezing which was hard to do at that point, so we were happy to be inside and staying for a little while. Never did I imagine how long "a little while" was going to be. We got set up on monitors and my hubby on his new pull-out bed, and I was texting and snapping photos with captions like "Last day pregnant!" "Can't wait for her to be here." My parents were driving down from PA tomorrow, and they would be here for her birth, and it would be such a wonderful thing. I kept looking at my husband thinking how exciting this would be and we would be smiling and crying and all this great stuff when she was born. The doctor came into see me and they gave me the induction instructions as well as options, and obviously I went with the one that seemed like it would work the best. We started the process, and I laid down to go to sleep, but it was the last thing I did.

Every time my daughter kicked or moved the monitor fell off, which meant a nurse coming in to say "hi, just me, what happened here?" At first it was cute, and I thought how wonderful it was to have this hands-on nursing staff so quick to tend to me. Fast forward about 8 hours of no sleep and that "Hi, what happened here?" got the response of "same shit as earlier Amy. I can't move, sleep, or do anything hooked up to these monitors." Peeing required me to unplug 19 things from me and the wall and it wasn't even worth going again. I just kept thinking "relax, this will all be different in the morning", and it sure was.

I was up literally all night staring out the window, looking at my peacefully sleeping husband and wanting to smother him with a pillow so he would have just a small inclination as to how pregnancy feels. He woke up around 9 when the doctor came in to check my progress, and I was so excited to see how far I dilated and what they were thinking was next. The doctor checked me and when she was finished explained to me that I was a little "softer" but no dilation. I looked at her and my husband and then said "wait, what? What does that mean? Did your little tablet not work? Give me another one." She explained that sometimes it does not go as planned. After a lot of discussions, and the nurses letting me know that I could just "go home" if I wanted, we decided to try again and continue with the process. No way was I going home after all of this shit. I wanted to meet my baby girl this weekend, and we were doing that one way or another.

The second attempt yielded the same result of no dilation whatsoever. I was really frustrated and feeling like my body sucked and was not working the way it should. I had to remind myself that my body is amazing and keeping this little girl safe and warm now. We consulted with the next on call doctor about the next steps which was to insert a balloon of some sort into my cervix, blow it up, and it would come out when I was about 4cm dilated. Not bad right? Wrong!! It was the most God-awful experience I had endured (to that point).

My parents had come into town anxiously awaiting the arrival of their first grandchild and they came to the hospital to check in. They were baffled that the induction was not working and trying to manage their own anxiety about being at the hotel, and how many more days would they need to extend the reservation. The nurses came in to prepare me for my "balloon" procedure and asked if I wanted a cocktail to help ease the pain. I have never been one to turn down a good cocktail, so I figured why not. She gave me a nice jab of nubane and in about 1 minute I felt like I was back in college. My parents were still there, and I almost felt guilty like I was high right in front of them. I was pretty sure this procedure was going to be rough, and result in my screaming and crying at some point so I asked them to just leave, and we would be in touch. I thank God every day I made that call because what happened next was something I don't think I have yet to recover from.

I was essentially flipped upside down with my lady parts in the air for the team of 5, yes 5 doctors and nurses to see and manipulate. One nurse stood by my side talking to me telling me how strong I was, and you know what? I have never forgotten about Mary. She knew exactly what I needed to hear in those very moments, and to remind me about the beautiful life growing inside of me. My husband was on the other side of me with a blank stare that I couldn't quite figure out. I wasn't sure if he was confused as to what was going on, or wondering how the hell I wasn't dead yet. After what felt like 6 hours, they finally inserted the balloon and brought me back down to eye level. They explained I may use the restroom and at any time if the balloon comes out to call the nurses because it means it worked. I prayed this would not be another failed attempt and it would cause some sort of dilation.

About an hour later I was 4cm dilated and they were able to start me on Pitocin. For the first 6 hours I was managing well and did not even think about an epidural as I closed my eyes and began to envision holding my baby girl soon enough. I figured I should rest because things may escalate quickly. About 3am on Sunday (day three) I woke up to shooting pains like my insides were on fire. For one second, I had forgotten I was pregnant and where I was, so I was deeply concerned with the pain; then it hit me, contractions were taking over. I jammed that nurse call button so fast and when she came in all I said was "epidural." I frantically woke my peacefully sleeping husband and let him know what I was opting to do. They brought the anesthesiologist in and ran down the hosts of dos and don'ts as I'm retaining none of this information and just trying to breathe. The nurse assumed her position and asked me to lean forward as far as I could, and they began the process. Although this did not hurt as bad as the balloon procedure, it was damn close, and the worst part was it happened twice because the first placement wasn't in the right spot. I about died during this procedure and remember my husband across the room just kind of standing in bewilderment. It was after all his 35th birthday and I can imagine that was not how he envisioned waking up.

After the epidural she informed me, they would be inserting a catheter and I would not be able to eat anything anymore. I wanted to fall on the floor and cry right then and there. I wish someone would tell me ahead of time, and I am sure that is what the anesthesiologist was mentioning when I was literally seeing red. She suggested I lay down and try and get some rest once the medications kick in, because it could be a long process. I guessed that Lisa had not seen my name on the delivery board for 3 days because I was the definition of a long process. I did manage to get some sleep and by the time I woke up the next morning I was 6cm dilated. I kept hoping for the best, but it never came. We decided that we would elect for a C section later in the evening so that we could meet our baby girl. I was not that upset about having the section because at about week 35 the baby girl was breech and I had to wrap my head around the idea that I would be having a section in order to safely deliver her. Sure, I wanted a vaginal birth so I could experience it all in that way, but little did I know having a section made me even tougher than I thought.

We called our families and let them know what would be happening and of course my parents came back to the hospital to check in before the procedure. My mom continued to remind me that a section is a great thing to have, and it does not make me less of a mom. I did appreciate those kind words because a lot of women are shamed for having sections. In my mind, I didn't care how it happened, I just wanted to see her. They began prepping me for surgery and explaining how things would happen and what to expect. They started to wean me off the pain meds so they could take me back and give me different medications. In that moment, everything went downhill quicker than the luge. The lady next to me went into labor requiring the doc, anesthesiologist, and nurses to rush in there and assist. One problem with that?? I had no pain medications for about 30 minutes. All of you "natural birth" mothers out there, my hat is off to you. I have no idea how the hell you did it, and I would never elect to feel that amount of pain again in my life. I was about to cut myself open and deliver my daughter right there in my bed. My husband finally found someone who came in and adjusted my medications and helped me relax. The only problem with that was that they flushed my IV so quickly I became super nauseous and was worried about puking.

This ladies labor was quick, and they were ready for me about 40 minutes after the ordeal started and I kissed my husband and said, "I'll see you back there." They wheeled me past my parents in the waiting room and I knew my mom was saying a rosary and my dad was praying to my Nana to keep me safe. I went into the operating room not knowing what would happen, so I had a few moments to myself with God. I asked him to give me and my husband strength, as well as to support and guide the doctor in delivering our baby. I asked God to please keep me safe and allow me to recover and meet my angel. My husband joined me, and we prayed together, then the surgery began. It felt like forever while it was going on, and all I could feel was some light pressure, and the smell of burning skin, which clearly was my own.

I heard the doctor say, "Ok there is the baby, and boy she was not going to come out on her own." I was waiting and waiting and then felt this intense pressure and the doctor said, "baby is out, baby is out" and then I heard nothing. I looked at my husband and said "what is wrong? Where is she and why is she not crying?" Before I could lift my head up and ask the doctor, I heard the most beautiful sound in all my life. I heard my daughter cry as she entered this world, and it was a moment I still reflect on and get teary eyed. She was perfect and had a head of hair which was so cool. My husband got to bring her over to me and we touched faces and I just cried looking at

her in complete and total awe at my Ava. My
baby was here, and my life is forever changed.
We got cleaned up and they wheeled us down the
hall and allowed my parents to visit us quickly.
Those moments are too precious for me to write
about, and if you have your own children you
understand, and if you don't you can only
imagine. Everyone shared embrace and then we
were whisked away to the recovery unit where in
my opinion, the shit was about to get real.

The Recovery

It was somewhere around 10:30 pm when
we arrived at the recovery unit at the hospital, and
I thought we would hand the baby over and get
some sleep until it was time to eat. The complete
and total opposite happened right after I received
a crash course in skin to skin and breastfeeding.
Remember, I had been in labor/induction mode
for 3 days and it was late in the evening after just
being cut open like birthday cake, so I was
exhausted. I was not even registering what the

nurse was saying to me other than "how is your pain?" That is a phrase I never want to hear again in my life after spending those 4 days in recovery. I attempted to breastfeed and did not do that well considering I didn't know what I was doing. It seemed like it was working and that she was eating, but honestly, what did I know?

The next couple of days were honestly the most difficult I had endured because I was laid up in bed with legs the size of tree trunks. A co-worker had told me to expect this and thank God she did because I could not get over what I looked like. I still looked like I was about 7 months pregnant and felt like I was hit by a bus. I had some gas pains that I was scared to let pass for the fear of ripping open my belly and uterus. Sleep was nonexistent for me and my husband who stayed on a pull-out chair!! Yes, a chair, it was not a couch just a long chair type thing that made sleeping in a jail cell seem appealing. Ava would wake up, cry, break loose from her swaddle and just continue to cry. This was not how I pictured it being once she was here and immediately, I began questioning myself as a mother, and if my body was designed for this. I felt unsure of everything going on around me and was trying to take the lead from the nurses and lactation specialists but between no sleep, pain meds, and complete confusion I was not sure which end was up at this point.

By day two I was begging the nurses to take my catheter out so I could get up and start moving. I know that you feel worse the longer you are laid up and not moving around after surgery, so I wanted to get up. Plus, I had not showered in 3 days, and I could not tell you the

last time I went a whole day without one. I felt
gross and kind of wanted to just see myself in the
mirror. The nurse obliged and was telling me
how I would feel weak and will need to take it
easy just standing up. Now remember, I am
strong, and worked out 90% of my pregnancy so I
knew what I was about to be facing, and I was not
going to let it get the best of me. Standing up felt
unsteady but so good as well. I managed to walk
to the bathroom, lower myself onto the toilet and
even get myself back up. I will spare you the
gory details of what came out of me and what I
was wearing as undergarments, but you can
imagine they were not pretty, nothing going on in
there was. The hospital was pretty smart and only
had mirrors that were from the neck and above, so
I had no real idea what my full body looked like,
but I almost didn't recognize my face. A friend of

mine told me that you will see yourself in a different way, and almost appear older after you have given birth. Right now, I totally got what she was saying. It wasn't as if I didn't like myself, but I saw myself as stronger than I had ever been, and a true warrior. That's it, I was a warrior!

We had some visitors over the next few days and people calling to check in on us, so we felt the love from everyone and were truly appreciative of this little gift. My husband is a second-time father, so I assumed he knew everything and was going to swoop in here and fix it all, but that was not the case either. I remember when he was first changing her and he said, "I am not even sure how to wipe her or clean her up." That was the first moment that I forgot all about the stress of what was going on, and stopped questioning myself and showed him how to clean up after a baby girl. It felt like the one and only task I did know how to complete. I was slowly feeling like myself after a few days and had some decent food in my system to make me really appreciate good food in life. Things seemed to have settled down and were shifting in a positive direction until they did her Billy Rubin test and found out she was jaundiced.

Those words cut through me in a way I didn't know were possible. Jaundiced? All I associated that with was that I was unable to care for my baby and it killed me. The nurse explained she wasn't getting what she needed from me, and we needed to supplement with formula. Oh my God!!! What?? What I heard was "Nicole, you're a shitty mom who never should have had a baby because your shitty body can't even produce enough nutrients to keep your daughter safe, so we are going to step in and take over." My world crashed and for the first time (of many to come) the tears wallowed up in my throat and then exploded down my face faster, and more uncontrolled than ever in my life. I felt like I failed, and it was only day 3. The crying was uncontrollable, and the poor nurse attempted to console me, but needed to get some food in my baby so she had to leave. My husband did a great job of reassuring me that it was natural, and unfair to him, he is a man, and his opinion and comfort did not much matter. I needed my mom! Then I thought, wait! She will think I am a failure too! I have never heard of people not being able to take care of their babies, what am I going to do?

I am very close to my mother, but we have always maintained the boundaries of mother and daughter. I consider her my best friend, my person, but have never shared those intimate details with one another, and that has always been a good thing. I called her crying hysterically and she simply listened. My mom said something to me in that moment that I have continued to carry with me. "Supplementing does not mean failing at all Nicole. If you were going to fail, God never would have tasked you with her life. Failing is not supplementing and letting her suffer." Two minutes later I had a whole new outlook on supplementing, and while I was still determined to breastfeed at some point, I knew I had to do what was best for now.

We used formula and I attempted to pump for the next two days, and then finally they decided they were ready to release us. I remember getting up and dressed that day looking at this little person like "how in the world did you live inside of me all of this time?" I put my pants on and as I tried putting my shoes on, I realized just how huge I was and that is when things started kicking in for real. My doctor came in and checked my incision and gave me the go ahead for stairs and all other things as well. I asked him when the swelling would go down and when he told me in 3-5 weeks I almost fell over. He reminded me that I had been on fluids for 6 days, 6 days!!! All that fluid had to go somewhere, and it sat in my legs and feet. I literally looked like the nutty professor; it was terrible. He suggested I walk and drink lots of water to speed the process up. We thanked him so much for bringing Ava to us safely and reminded me to set up an appointment in a few weeks. We got our baby girl dressed and headed home! I remember thinking how I cried some time at the hospital and how that must be what post-partum feels like. I remember thinking it sucked and wasn't a good feeling, but at least it's behind me.

"Oh, my dear, it is ever so right in front of

you"

Returning Home

When I tell you that if it were not for my
husband, I probably would not have made it
through this portion of the event. When we were
driving home all I kept thinking about was how
uncomfortable I was, and I just wanted to use the
bathroom and get Ava to take a nap. I still dream
about doing those things to this day, but they
occur in a much different mindset. This was by

far the most challenging chapter of my life, and while I knew that it was not going to be easy, I did not realize how under discussed this really is in a community of beautiful women. Women have babies and have been for literally the beginning of time. Women are also forced to endure changes to their bodies both physically and emotionally all while having to be quiet about what was REALLY going on in there. I decided I would not stay quiet because I was not ashamed of what happened, what I felt, and why I wanted to talk about it.

The second we walked through the door the house did not feel the same to me. I saw everything in my house as a potential disaster for my daughter. Then I saw them, the stairs. Now I know the doctor encouraged me to do them, but if I wanted to get from the front door into the living room, I was going to have to get my ass there myself. I was not going to have my husband throw his back out while trying to lug me up the steps. It was a reality check to realize that I would probably crush my husband if I landed on him, and that was not going to benefit anyone of us at this time. I got up the steps and felt like I deserved some type of medal for that. I had to drag my legs up, and take a break halfway, but I got there. That was the first of many humbling events for me this year, and one of the biggest achievements as well.

Anyone who knows me knows I was adamant about unpacking and starting a wash. It was great that I had goals, but none of that was going to happen anytime soon. My husband took everything upstairs and said "I'll take care of it" which you can understand gave me severe anxiety, but I replied "sounds great" all while sweating and thinking how he will destroy all our clothes and belongings in the first 48 hours. He moved right from his parents' house in with me a few years ago, so the laundry thing never really had to get learned, and boy was he about to get a crash course. My daughter was asleep in her car seat, so I dragged myself up the steps and taught him in 15 minutes how to do the laundry and begged him to throw a load in now. Knowing me inside and out and obliged and I started to relax.

Since I was so relaxed it hit me! I was finally able to use the bathroom and I was so happy about that. It had been days and I felt like that was contributing to my irritability and overall discomfort, so I was excited. My husband decided to jump in the shower and in that moment, I was like "omg! Ava" I went back down the steps like a snail and found her still sleeping peacefully in her car seat (Thank God). Now, how was I supposed to use the bathroom and keep an eye on her? Obviously, she had to come in with me, but I can't lift her so now what??? I thought I was going to implode right there so I slid her car seat with my foot near the door and went inside to handle my business. I hadn't been home for an hour, and I already had company with me in the bathroom. I prayed my husband didn't come out of the shower to find me in a compromising situation, door open and all.

Then the unsettling reality that this was going to be my new norm was slowly starting to sink in, especially when I hooked myself up to the breast pump for the first time, turned that sucker on and felt my nipples get set on fire. Yes, I became familiar with the pump before I had the baby, but how familiar can you really get? Well, I started off like a rock star and was set on producing whatever I could to keep baby girl full and happy, and we would supplement with formula when needed to. Formula, yes, that stuff we did not have at the house because I never thought we would need it. How were we going to get that stuff? My husband was about to leave me all alone with our newborn and go get formula, and I was totally shit scared.

Who is scared to be alone with their own child? What was wrong with me? I couldn't help thinking something would happen to her and I would not know what to do with her, or how to help her if I was left all alone. We chatted for a little bit and my husband reminded me that I was her mother, and if anyone knew what to do to care for her it was me. Great pep talk baby, but I was petrified. Thankfully she slept the entire time he was gone which felt like 4 days, but in all actuality, it was 45 minutes. Ok, now that everyone is home, we can game plan what our days and evenings are going to look like for the next couple of weeks. My plan was to pump every 2-3 hours and just start stockpiling as fast as I could, and at nighttime he would feed her formula.

I was pretty blessed having my husband home with me for 4 weeks. 4 full weeks he was devoted to taking care of me and little Ava. Some of you may be wondering why I didn't call on my mom and other supports and that was because me and my husband wanted time to bond with Ava, as well as learn to lean on each other during this time and strengthen our bond. It was hard for me to tell everyone "Thanks, but not right now", but in the end I am glad we did choose this path we did. Strengthening our relationship is exactly what we did, and almost by having it completely broken. I thank God every day for the man he put in my life to be my partner, because unlike a lot of women before me, and even friends, my husband sees me as an equal, and we partnered together to care of our daughter during the first month of her life.

I remember going to bed the first night and crawling under the sheets and thinking I would be happy with just one hour of sleep tonight. That never even happened, and not because of Ava but because my body was so friggen sore in so many different areas I didn't think I would survive the night. I laid down and immediately the weight of my belly started suffocating me, so I moved onto my side. Nope! Those hips were still sensitive and sore, and I could forget about sleeping on my stomach. I went to get up out of bed to figure out what I was going to do, and realized I couldn't physically sit up. It may have been because I was tired, or the fact I had zero core strength at this time, but I could not do it. My husband came over and helped me up and then I bawled my eyes out on the edge of the bed. It was the ugly uncontrollable balling where you can't breathe or see, and it seems like none of the tears will stop. He attempted to console me yet again, and it was no use. I felt broken. I felt used up and abused and felt that there was no way I was going to be able to do any of this.

We talked for a bit before feeding Ava and thought about the two of us sleeping downstairs on the reclining couches or moving a recliner into our room and my husband said "You go downstairs and sleep. I got this." I have never enjoyed hearing such words come out of his mouth as I did in that moment. I hugged him, kissed Ava, and went downstairs. Of course, I laid reclined on the couch, but I was able to get up by myself and move around some. I remember closing my eyes at 11pm and waking up at 4 to pump. Then he brought Ava down to me, asked if I was ok, and then he went upstairs to try and get some sleep himself. This is how our relationship was for the next 4 weeks. We barely saw one another, and I know he didn't sleep much, but I was sleeping which meant I was producing great amounts of breastmilk and Ava was getting bigger and stronger each day.

My husband is an incredible man! Yes, we have our moments, and there are days I give him a hard time for not doing more for our family, but I stand firm that without his support and willingness to suffer from sleep deprivation, our daughter would not have had the nutrients from her mother that she needed, and I probably would have fared a lot worse in this situation. I could never thank him or give him enough credit for all that he did for us. He worked the overnight shift feeding Ava every 2 hours without complaining once. I am not saying this to make anyone jealous or feel shitty about themselves, but simply to say you NEED your husband to be your partner. As much as it killed me that we had to supplement, and that she wouldn't latch, I realized that it probably saved me in a lot of ways, and allowed for the two of them to bond, and him to support me every day. Ladies, introduce a bottle as soon as you can, so even if it is just two hours of uninterrupted sleep you get, at least it is something. Communicate to your partner what you need in those early weeks, and be kind to one another, it sucks! There were plenty of times that I lost my shit on him and could not even explain why. He was doing so much for us, yet I found opportunities to remind him what I went through and how it is not easy on me. Come to think of it, I probably should have found a support group for him, but that was the furthest thing from my mind.

Coming to Terms

Emotions are high, and you cannot control how you are feeling even when you know that it is silly, and you are going to be ok. I remember calling my parents one night while I was hooked up to the pump, and my dad answered the phone and said "Hey Cole! How are you buddy? Everything ok?" I almost died at the sound of his voice. I reverted to a little girl who wanted her daddy there with her helping her through this big thing that was going on. I knew

if I broke down it would have broken his heart, so

I swallowed hard and said, "hey dad, yep, things

are ok, just trying to adjust". He laughed a little

and then I said, "please get mom". My mom got

on the phone and said, "hey kiddo" and I

immediately lost it. I cried so hard and was so

open with her about how I was so upset and had

no clue why. She said "it's post-partum Cole.

Cry, and get it out, but then put your big girl pants

on and get back to it."

Those words: post-partum hit me like a

ton of bricks. Not me! I am not depressed! I am a

mental health professional with a PhD in human

behaviors, I know the signs and symptoms of

depression and it is not happening to me. It was.

I was just like every person I tell people not to be.

Do not deny yourself help and treatment simply

because you want to appear like everything is fine. That is what I was doing. I was pretending that everything was fine because it was only week two and I felt like I was falling apart. I am not supposed to be depressed until well into her time on Earth is all I kept thinking. Where did I get this from? There is no timeframe for depression, much like there isn't for grief, but I was putting pressure on myself and doing one thing I said I never would, and that was judge myself. How do I overcome this depression without seeking clinical help (because I surely didn't have time for that, and my pride wouldn't let me). So, I cried. I cried every single day for the next few weeks, but it was like a workout to me. I got up, got it over with, kissed my baby and got on with my day. Some days I cried a few times, and I always did it in the same place…the bathroom. One day it got so bad I had to pull myself off the bathroom floor, look in the mirror and beg God for the strength to go care for my baby.

This was an emotional couple of weeks for me, and trying to hide it was even worse. Do not hide it! Talk about it. Call a friend, call your mom, and call me to cry out loud but talk about it. Make it real. We hide this so much because we are supposed to be strong, but guess what? We are stronger than we think, and God chose us as the gender to carry and sustain life, so if we want to feel depressed about our new lives, we are more than entitled to do so, and I am no longer apologizing for it. I started to feel a little bit better about things and was being very open about how I was feeling, but only to my husband and my mother. My mom should have been psychiatrist in another life because that woman is simply amazing. You know how God chooses your mom for you as your angel on this earth? Well, I hit the lottery when it came to choosing mine! My mom was my lifeline for a lot of this stuff, and never once did she tell me to suck it up, or I was just experiencing what everyone else has before me. She told me to get it out, and address it, and talk to her about it. She was understanding, supportive, and saved me in a way I could never fully explain.

I never thought about killing myself, but I did wonder what life would be like without me in it. I wondered if insurance money would be better than my income, and if someone else could do a better job than I could raising my daughter. My thought process was totally fucked up, and I can't believe I even thought that way for a moment, but these hormones and emotions are a total bitch that take over all your rational thoughts. I would NEVER leave this earth on my own accord, and Ava needs me in her life more than anyone else. I helped create her so I would never turn my back on her, ever. I decided to become closer with my baby every day, so I had that reason right in front of me at all times. I wanted to be here, I wanted to be her mom, and I wanted to beat whatever the hell was attempting to take me down, and I would overcome these feelings.

Four weeks went by faster than anything I had encountered in my life, and my husband was about to go back to work. Then it hit me again. I am going to be alone with Ava and solely responsible for her. How am I going to work the night and day shift, and pump, and do all of this by myself? The answer was simple, I had to do it and find a way to do it because I am her mother, and I can do anything when it comes to her. By this point I had re-entered the bedroom (thank God) and never realized how much I missed sleeping next to my husband, snoring and all. It made me feel like we were husband and wife again, and not just two people switching responsibilities off each day. We also talked about what I needed mentally and physically moving forward and if I was ok to be by myself. Of course, I was not, but did not want to admit it. I remember wanting to be able to do it all by myself and not need help but why? Why? Because society wants us to think it is possible. Guess what? It is not possible, and it is a form of torture that is not necessary for a woman who just went through a miracle.

It is not a sign of weakness to want or need help. I truly believe denying yourself those supports is the weaker of the two. Childbirth and bringing baby home should be a supportive, loving, nurturing time for a new mom and we need to do better as women to make sure that is happening for ourselves, our sisters, our friends and just women in general. We need to be more supportive rather than shaming and reach out to one another rather than avoidant because you don't want to intrude. Intrude in one another's lives and insert yourself into someone's life so that they truly know you are there for them. I will say that I had three friends in my life who consistently reached out to me, and told me things would be ok, and asked if I needed anything. They were also my sounding board for questions like "is her poop normal? Have you thought about killing your husband? Is it normal to want to go on vacation without anyone? Am I a bad mom if…" Now don't get me wrong. I had plenty of resources and friends that I reached out to for advice, but these three women sought me out. They inserted themselves in my life just to simply say "I know it's, hard and I remember how I felt. I am here for you no matter what. Remember, you will make it through this." For obvious reasons they will remain nameless, but they know exactly who they are. I remember thinking back to those early weeks and those awful feelings of not being enough and I realized I knew exactly what I needed to not go back to that dark place, MOM.

Calling for Help

I had about 5 days alone with Ava under my belt, so it wasn't as though I "couldn't" do this, but it was tough trying to do it all. I remember telling my husband I think I want my mom to visit and help me out while he adjusts back to work, and he was like "sure." Then I told him "Like for 3 weeks." Again, he did not fight me on this like most men would. Who wants their mother-in-law at their house for 3 weeks??? He never batted an eye about it, an again, it was because he knows me, and knew exactly what I needed: Love and support from the most important woman in my life. So, I picked up the phone, called home and said "Hey, want to visit, like for 3 weeks?" My mother's immediate response was "Mommy's on her way." You know how that made me feel? Like everything was going to be ok. Who cares that I am 35, with my own child, but knowing my mom was coming for weeks was incredible and made me feel so safe. We worked out the logistics and she talked to my dad about it because heck, he was going to be without his wife for 3 weeks. All jokes aside, that was a tough sacrifice to ask them to make, and I'm sure they talked about how important it was, but my parents are amazing people!

That first week before my mom came, she talked to me about breastfeeding and asked if I had tried to get her to latch at all again. I told her I felt stressed and judged so I didn't really try because I was too anxious. She told me to take Ava upstairs all by myself and try to get her to latch. I was so hesitant to do this because I did not want to fail again at this. My mom assured me that I would be fine, and we may be able to do it now that we are alone. I went upstairs and we tried, and we latched. I felt like I just hit the lottery with this progress. After all of this time and hoping and praying I was able to sit calmly with my baby and feed her from my breast. I could not believe what was happening. It was not totally easy by any means, and we had to keep adjusting each time we did it, but we got to a place where she was being exclusively breast fed, plus one bottle at night from daddy.

My mom and dad came down the day before Ava turned one month and spent some time with me and my husband, and then my dad headed back to Pennsylvania leaving his wife, daughter, and granddaughter in Maryland. My mom and I talked a lot about what I needed, and how she planned to help with it. She was basically going to hang out with Ava so I could shower and eat, and obviously do a lot of bonding. I was so excited for my mom to spend time with my daughter and was looking forward to catching up with her myself since we don't get to see one another as often as we should, or would like to.

The next couple of weeks were very eye opening for me regarding what it takes to develop a bond with your little one, and how incredibly amazing it was to watch my mom in her new role as Nonna to my baby. Every morning I would take Ava downstairs and my mom would be on the couch having her coffee and absolutely light up when we came in the room. I would hand Ava over to her and pour myself a giant cup of coffee as well. My mom would start talking to Ava and asking her all about her night, and what she had planned for the day, and I would just watch and catch up on social media. I thought it was so cool they were building their own bond, and I enjoyed watching it unfold right in front of me.

We had a lot of girl time jam packed into those 2.5 weeks of Nonna visiting and I wouldn't have traded any of it for the world. I watched my mom bond with my daughter, husband, and stepson during this time. She cooked amazing meals (as always) and took such a burden off me without ever feeling like she was being overwhelmed. Each night when my husband came home from work, my mom would hang out to say hi, and then retreat to our finished basement where she could relax all while respecting our family time too. We had a well working system in place and as happy as I was, I was sad to know that it would not be like this forever. It was great to sit on the couch, make meals, and catch up with my mom in new ways each day. I wanted and wished so bad her, and my dad would just move closer.

We took advantage of having help during this time and sought out to interview daycare providers. Talk about the most intense and scary type of interviews you will ever go on. I was trusting someone with my own little life outside of my body. I cried just thinking about Ava being in someone else's care and not getting the attention she needed from them. Those thoughts began to haunt me and kept me up a lot at night. She was so tiny and defenseless anything could happen to her, and I would make sure it never did…but could I?

When the day came that my dad was coming back to get my mom it was bittersweet. It was great to see my dad gain, and he could not get over how much Ava had changed and how big she was getting. He stayed with us one night, and they were ready to head back the next day. It broke my heart to have them leave, but I knew it had to be done. I had gotten the guidance and support from my mom that I needed to fully embark on this new journey as a mother. My father couldn't get over how I was as a mother, and shared how proud he was, and how incredible it was to see me as a mom. The three of us shared a tearful goodbye and huge hugs in the garage that morning, and I went back into my house to cuddle Ava. I spent a lot of time crying that morning, happy tears, sad tears, scared tears, but I also explained to Ava what an incredible woman her Nonna was.

.

The Second Month

As I mentioned in the beginning, I was very blessed to have the support of my husband and my family during this time of transition for me. My husband would be off for two more weeks in about two weeks or so, leaving me two weeks of just me and Ava time, and that my friends is where a lot of emotions, resentment, and all out wars began for me. I enjoyed the time with my daughter so much, but it was during this time I realized that I could not do it all by myself. My husband's job is demanding, and on top of an hour commute he left me at 7am and coming back between 6 and 7pm each night. I would be starving and not able to make myself too many meals unless I did everything on a scheduled rotation which was challenging. I really had to wait for Ava to sleep in order to be able to shower, eat, make a meal, and oh yea, take a nap myself. I would get up a few times during the night with her to nurse and then she would wake up super early in the morning to start her day.

This was also the month where I received clearance to start working out again and was thrilled to be able to do this. I have an amazing sisterhood of women who have connected virtually and support one another through out workout team, and I was so excited to jump back in rather than watching from the sidelines. These

ladies were an amazing support system for me all
through my pregnancy and delivery and we were
all anxious for me to get back into things. I was
so pumped and so ready that I jumped in full force
and realized I couldn't do shit. When I got
pregnant I was doing push-ups and planks and
moves that you wouldn't believe, and now here I
was 6 weeks pp and I couldn't push my fat ass off
the ground. Yes, fat ass was what I referred to
myself as and all the negative self-talk began.

I was so mean to myself after just
having delivered a healthy, beautiful baby out of
this body I was calling fat. I didn't give my body
any credit for the strength it used during the
delivery and afterwards, every time I had to move
up the steps or pick my daughter up. Why was I
so hard on myself? I did it because I was upset
that I wasn't where I was 40 weeks ago and didn't

realize I never again would be in that place. Ava was pretty good for the first week and I had a good little thing going where I would work out and shower after her 9am feeding because that was when she took her longest nap. For one week I felt like the old Nicole with a workout routine and all. The following week that all came crashing down because those long naps turned into cat naps, and never again was I able to sneak in a workout.

Now, a lot of people (myself included at one point) would give me shit for not being able to find time to work out, but it was true. The down time that I did have I wanted to sit alone and just contemplate where I was in life. The time I had alone and "free" was me catching up on everything else in life in a mere 30 minutes that my daughter slept. I kept telling myself that when my husband came home in the evening, I would at least get 20 minutes in on the treadmill; sadly that never happened either. I finally came to terms that I would not be returning to my fitness lifestyle anytime soon, and that meant this body had to wait as well. One of my girlfriends told me after I had Ava, "Be kind to yourself, and give yourself a whole year to get back into things." At the time I thought she was nuts, but now I see how smart she is.

The kinder I am to myself, and the more that I cut myself a break for where I am, the better I feel, and in turn the healthier I am. I began just focusing on eating correctly and getting good fuel in my system for Ava, and for me as well. The days I wasn't sleeping so well were even more important for me to get the necessary food into my body, and water, water is the most important thing (other than Ava) in my life at this moment. I could drink 4 gallons of water a day while nursing her and trying to stay fit. At this time, I was adjusting again, and finding my new normal with Ava. I did not have my mom, and for the most part I had my husband for an hour or so in the evenings, and all weekend too.

Things started getting rough when I was alone for so long, and I tried to tell him how hard it was, but I am convinced that men just think we are built for this shit. Yes, we are, but that does not mean we don't want some support and just someone to take everything else off our plate. My husband does most of the cleaning in the house (the bathrooms) and our house duties were not getting done because of our new normal. It took everything I had to use spare time to dust my house. My parents offered to pay a cleaning person to come in and do a deep clean, but he refused. He fought me on this topic for months to come, and well, you'll see how that plays out. I just never understood why men just don't say "sure honey. You endured so much for this family so whatever it is that you want, you let me know." Any men out there picking up this book I strongly encourage that you insert that phrase somewhere in your vocabulary very soon.

The end of my maternity leave was fast approaching, and my husband and I agreed before Ava was born that he would break his paternity leave up into two parts. He took 4 weeks up front when Ava was born, and he would take the last two weeks off during my final two weeks of leave. This left us time to re-connect as a family, and for him to support me during the transition to her daycare provider. I will tell you this, it was one of the smartest things we had done up to this point. I never realized preparing to go back to work would be so difficult and require so much from me in a short amount of time. I also had no idea how things were going to go with Ava going to daycare. We found a wonderful daycare provider who met all our expectations, and we were hopeful things would go well when we introduced Ava to her. There is no better feeling as a new mom than just have that feeling in your gut that your child is going to be cared for in the best way possible when you are not around. During the last two weeks we really spent time hanging around the house, catching up on ironing, laundry, and snuggle time with Ava. That first week flew by, and before we knew it Ava was going to be starting daycare that Monday.

Anyone who knows me knows that I never return to work on a Monday. Even during vacation, I will intentionally take the following Monday off so I can return on Tuesday. I never enjoyed Mondays, and quite honestly who wants to go back to work for a full week after being off. My situation was different this time around since I went out on leave on a Thursday, it meant I would be returning to work on a Thursday which was just fine with me for my first week back. We got some good advice to start Ava in daycare that week so we knew what to expect and what adjustments we needed to make at home so we could get to work on time. I didn't realize what a crucial piece of advice it was for us to do this until that Monday came. Sure, I was prepared, and I knew that she needed to go to daycare, but with every fiber of my being I wanted to quit my job and stay home with her forever. I never understood women who stayed at home with their kids. I could never grasp not wanting to go into an office and work all day. That was, until I had Ava. I had just spent 11 weeks with this little piece of me, and now we had to separate. Just now when things were getting fun, and she was smiling at me, and laughing and doing all sorts of cool stuff, we had to be apart? It was soul crushing to say the least.

Monday morning, we got up, showered, dressed and took some pictures. I remember putting Ava in her car seat and just starting to cry uncontrollably. The feeling was horrible, and I felt like the worst mom in the world. I expected to be sad, but I was feeling guilty, sad, miserable, and like I was not enough for her. I was crushed that I was crying and in front of my baby girl who had no idea why her mommy was crying. I wiped my face, smiled, and said, "mommy loves you more than you will ever know" and kissed my daughter all over her face. My husband asked if I was ok and reminded me how strong I was. Great, because weak and shameful were the only feelings I was associating myself with in the moment. We got her in the car and drove over to daycare which seemed like a two-minute ride. Right before we got out of the car, I told him I couldn't do it. I said I wanted to take her home and I would figure it out from there. He held my hand, and told me that was not realistic, and that we would be sad, but she would be ok.

We got out of the car and got Ava into the daycare provider's home. She was awake and looking around at her new surroundings. The guilt was boiling in my throat to the point I thought I would throw up all over the place. We chatted about her likes and dislikes and the moment she looked at Ava was priceless. "She is so beautiful" is all she kept saying to us. I passed Ava to her father in the hopes it made me feel less like I was abandoning my child, and then he gave her to her daycare provider. In that moment everything changed. My daughter took to this woman like nothing I could have imagined. She cozied right up on her chest and made herself comfortable without a single peep. She was ok, and she was going to be ok. It was 100 times harder on me than it was on her. She didn't think I was abandoning her; it was all in my head and what I thought she was going to think. We left a few minutes later and again; I lost it in the driveway. My husband hugged me and told me to be strong and that Ava was in great hands. We left and went to the movies that day to keep our minds off Ava, and it worked. We picked our little girl up that afternoon and received raving reports of how amazing she was. On the plus side, she did not seem to have forgotten me, or hated me for leaving her there. Day 1 was over, and I was relieved we survived.

Taking my daughter to daycare the rest of the week and even into the second week was some of the hardest days I have had. Everyone tells you how rough it will be, and tries to normalize it, but until you experience it you have no clue how much your heart attempts to break during those hours. Sure, it got easier each time I took her, and she started to get comfortable going over there. We sent her with some of the things she really liked, and the first blanket she slept with when home from the hospital. Maybe it did not matter much, but in my head, it was her little

piece of home that went with her every day, and

that made me feel good.

Returning to Work

The dreaded day had come! I had to go back to work. Now, I really enjoy my job, and work at a wonderful agency that has been very accommodating to many folks before me. I did not worry about a thing while I was on leave and knew that everything would be handled, and I would get back into the swing of things in no time. The one area that scared me the most was how I had changed as a person. I used to have a fiery personality, so much so I got some good feedback from my supervisor about building better working relationships etc. and I made those conscious changes. I worried that I had become soft and would not be able to follow through on things as I once had. I was on email all the time and tended to over work when "off the clock" at home. It was just something that was in me, and now I wondered if I still had it. I never could have imagined all of the things that were going to change or require me to approach at a different angle now having Ava in my life. One of the scariest parts of going back to work...pumping on the clock.

Day one started off with breakfast off site with two co-workers who covered for me while I was on leave. We caught up over eggs and coffee, shared some laughs, some stories, and I shared some tears. I am a sensitive person, always have been and always will, but this post-partum stuff had me crying like a baby over stupid things. The best part about where I work is there are a lot of moms who have been through this as well, and some more recent than others. My closest co-worker has a son who is roughly 8 months older than Ava so naturally she was my go-to in a lot of situations during pregnancy, and I imagined it would carry through to this time as well.

After breakfast I needed to get to my office so that I could, uh, pump. My goodness! You want to talk about anxiety provoking feelings? Trying to schedule pumping into my schedule was tough, and I needed to be as open as I could be with people so that they didn't think I was blowing off their meetings, or taking three lunch breaks a day. I felt like if I was open about it, people would be more understanding, and they were. The first two days of pumping were tough. I was just sitting there holding these cups and milk pouring into them while I looked blankly at a computer screen feeling like a prisoner. It was in those moments I thought there was no way I could carry on with pumping while working. I shared my sentiments with two co-workers, and they very boldly asked "Why are you holding the cups?" I explained I didn't have a hands-free pump, so I had no choice. They almost died at my response. This is one of those moments where you are glad you overshare because I was about to get some kick ass advice that would forever change my pumping life. "Nicole, you can purchase a hands-free bra that allows you to pump and still be able to use your hands." I almost fell over when I heard this. WHAT??? This would have been great information to have about 3 months ago! Jesus Christ why doesn't anyone talk about this shit? I looked it up on the web and sure as shit, there it was, staring me in the face. The hands-free breast pump bra (aka…my lifesaver). I ordered that sucker up with two-day shipping and was excited for Monday to get here so I could pump freely!

All I wanted to do when the weekend came was to sleep and hang out with Ava, and I did everything but that. We had a busy weekend with visitors and catching up with housework. It was hard to try and cram everything into the weekend all while trying to get some sleep too. Being a nursing, working mother was a lot harder than I thought it was, and not as easy for my husband to see and understand that. I did all the laundry, dusted the house, nursed, and fed my daughter, bathed her, got groceries, cooked and meal prepped for the following week. All that shit together should have allowed me to sleep for a whole day, but it didn't happen, and neither did a nap. Before I knew it, Sunday was over, and I was preparing for my first full week to return to work. How the hell am I going to do this is the only thought that consistently ran through my head.

Monday came in like a ton of bricks, and one awful surprise showed up with Monday…my period. What in the fuck? I couldn't catch a break these days. All the girls I knew who breastfed told me how great it was for me to do this, and the natural benefits for Ava as well as me such as help losing the weight, and no period. Ha! That was a crock of shit because I got my period, and after not having it for close to 14 months that bitch came in hard! I had to go to CVS and buy Pads. Something no one wants to tell you is after you have a baby, using a tampon is not that great of an experience. Sure, I had a c-section so what should that matter, however, things still were not the same down there and tampons were not a friend of mine now. As if returning to work, maintaining a home, and caring for my daughter wasn't enough, how about adding extreme blood loss to that mess? I would look up at God and just smile some days because all that got me through this was the thought that he knew just how strong I was.

I started to get into a good routine at work with pumping, eating, and working at all designated times. I never really took a lunch break before, and sure wasn't planning on it now. I was making my lunches the night before in an attempt to eat healthy, and save some money. I was equipped with my own new office that did not have any windows either. Pre Ava, I would have really balked at this, and pretty sure I had a lot to say about it before I went on maternity leave. When I look at it now, I am so happy there are no windows because it is one less area of concern for me when I am pumping. Another great thing is that I only have a key to this office. At my old office everyone had one standard key that opened everyone's office, so at any point you could be in there taking a nap and people would just let themselves in. Talk about anxiety provoking for new mothers who were attempting to pump during their lunch break. I also was equipped with my new "hands free bra" that made me feel unstoppable at still being connected to my work while pumping for Ava. One of my co-workers gave me a do not disturb sign to put up while pumping because surely that would keep people away.

It was about my third day at work when things took a turn for the worse, and one poor decision could have led me to lose my job. Now, without the window, and the key issues, I still had anxiety that there would be a fire, and someone would come breaking down my door, exposing my boobs and milk for all to see. I know it seems ridiculous, but until you are in that vulnerable position at work you cannot judge me for my thoughts. I put my sign up, locked my door, and began pumping in the afternoon when it seemed like no one was in the building. About halfway through my pump session I could hear someone knocking on the doors in the hallway, getting no response, and then a key going into these doors. "Ok, relax Nicole, someone probably left a key for someone so they could use their office." A minute later, the same sound, a door closer to mine. Now, I am starting to panic assuming someone is going to knock on my door and then put a key in and attempt to open my door. "Wait a second, they can't do that because they don't have a key, and I have my do not disturb sign up." WRONG!! Not a moment later and there is a knock on my door. I decided to sit quietly because I have my sign up and they should know not to disturb me. They knocked again and I couldn't really hear anything, so I just yelled out "I'm busy" and started to sweat profusely. Then, they put a key in the door and started turning the knob. I almost shit my pants! I couldn't stop pumping because this is liquid gold, but I couldn't be exposed either. I threw a shawl over myself opened the door in haste and said "WHAT??" It was a maintenance tech and he said "Oh my bad" as he could see something clearly was not right. I told him I had the sign up for a reason and he needed to respect that and not knock. He ran away from my door before we could say anymore.

I sat back down at my desk and was shaking. Someone almost caught me in my most vulnerable position and I had all the protections in place (locked door, sign up) and it still didn't matter to people. What was the problem? Why was there no respect for what someone was doing behind a closed door? I didn't think I needed to tell people what I was doing in there, whether it be by mouth, or a sign that said, "do not disturb I am pumping milk out of my breasts for my daughter." I realized, yes, I should be more open about this and then maybe people will be more respectful of what is going on. The next day I tracked down this guy and had a conversation with him about why I use that sign. He still looked mortified and apologized over and over for coming to the office like that. I explained to him I have a new baby at home and nurse in my office on occasion. He seemed to understand my position and we had never had another encounter like that to date.

It got me thinking about why were aren't more open and honest about what we are doing, especially as women returning to work after having a baby. I feel like a lot of women before me were going through the same sort of issues, but they stayed hidden about them and the effect they were having on them. Being a working mom is hard. Being a working mom of a newborn that you are pumping breastmilk for is super hard. When things get hard it is helpful to have support in place to assist us in staying functional, especially at work. Times have changed folks.

Not too many women can stay home and care for their children the way our mothers did, and although I would love it, we need two incomes. With those changes at home come changes at work. Changing the way we schedule things, the way we talk about things, and the events we can and cannot attend. There were a lot of "I'm sorry, I can't make that meeting" or a few "I will have to call in for that" and one or two stern "No, I cannot adjust my schedule for this today." I never realized the amount of planning that was going to have to happen in all aspects of my life when I decided to continue to breastfeed while I worked, and it never really got easier.

It was quite interesting to me that every time I mentioned having to pump while at work, I did it with a face on, or an eye roll, and every time that happened my husband reverted to his key phrase of "We could just give her formula." I wasn't sure how many more times I could hear that phrase come out of his mouth before I poured formula directly in it myself. He was doing more harm than good, and he just could not see it. I had told him several times before that making that comment is not helpful. He felt like he had to remind me of the formula, so I didn't keep "pressuring" myself to breastfeed. What he didn't realize is that I didn't want any commentary from him other than a simple "Baby, you are doing amazing. I don't know how you do it, but I admire your strength in continually caring for our daughter when it is tough on you." Yes, I realize that is unrealistic to expect that response but shit, some days that is ALL I wanted to hear him say. I finally told him I never wanted to hear the formula phrase again, and from that day on he never did. I know he struggled understanding my decision to breastfeed Ava while I worked if it was "so hard", but the truth was, it wasn't that it was hard, it was just something extra that I had to do at work that reminded me I was a mother, and a damn good one.

I started to realize that while I was at work, I was doing pretty good juggling everything, but when I got home after work with Ava, that is when it was really challenging. She was not independent, so I had to take her everywhere I went, and that limited me to not being able to work out if she was awake, not being able to clean out her bottles and all my breastfeeding gear when I got home, and sometimes not even being able to cook dinner. I had to keep her entertained unless she took a nap. As I have said, my husband has put a lot of late nights into work, and while we agreed this was going to stop, it hadn't yet and I was riding the struggle bus hard, and alone. My duties as a wife started to fail miserably, and I was lucky if I made dinner one or two nights a week, and that made me feel guilty. Guilty huh? I work all day, care for our daughter before and after work, and during, and my husband works late. Why did I feel guilty? Did he feel guilty that I was not eating dinner until he came home around 7:30pm? Did he feel guilty that I was unable to produce enough milk somedays because I didn't have time to cook or eat, and when I started to eat guess who else got hungry…Ava. It was during this stretch of adjusting to work life balance that I began to resent him for being able to do whatever he wanted without what seemed like a single care in the world.

As moms we must always put our needs behind us. Yes, as moms, not as dads, as moms. We are the sole provider for our babies at that very early stage, and dad gets to do whatever he wants because he knows that mom will be there. I ate alone, on the floor, and had cold dinners many nights while he worked late. He never complained there wasn't a meal when he got home, but he never held me and told me he was so sorry I was doing this all by myself. This was not what I had signed up for in our marriage. I did not choose to be a single mother during the week with a new baby, but here I was, alone and not happy about it one bit. The funny thing about having a baby is that it will teach you how much shit you are capable of, and how much shit you are willing to tolerate from other people. I am capable of way more than I ever imagined, and there was nothing I wouldn't do for my heartbeat. I also learned that I would tolerate a lot from my husband because I loved him, but there would come a breaking point, and one he probably wouldn't see coming.

We argued a lot my first month back at work. We argued about everything, and mostly his desire to pour more of himself into his job than into his family. Everyday felt like Groundhog Day for a while. I got up, took care of Ava, showered with the baby monitor, fixed her bottles, packed my lunch, got her in the car and off to daycare. Worked all day, pumped, picked her up, came home washed everything out (including dirty clothes of hers) attempted to make a meal, stay awake, eat, and feed her all before he walked in the door between 7 and 8pm each night. It was wreaking havoc on me emotionally, physically, and spiritually,

constantly questioning "Is this the life I want?" I

begged him every day to come home early but

focus on us rather than your job. Each time he

would tell me "I will, I hear you" and each day I

trusted him less and less. We were heading down

a dark path, and I was the only one with a

flashlight to see what was coming, he was blind.

Losing Control

I knew as well as anyone else that things could not continue going the way they were and I was going to have to suck it all up for a while, or there would be huge problems looming all around the place. A lot of challenges arose during the next two months while I was still at work. I have a stepson who I love and adore, and he was struggling with a lot during this time. There is not much I am willing to share surrounding the ins and outs with him, but there was tremendous strain on me and my husband's relationship due to several factors out of our control, and our stepson needed us in a way we were not prepared for. In essence, I became a "new mom" to a newborn and a 14-year-old at the same time, and it overwhelmed me to my core. There were days when I wanted to leave this life (not by death) but just pick up and start off somewhere else. The old PP Depression feelings started to sink back in, and there were days when I didn't feel like I had much support or backing from my husband and it was crushing. I didn't know which way to turn in our marriage, and other than praying to God so hard for so long I chose to bottle up a lot of feelings.

I didn't feel heard by my husband, and a lot of this was hormonal, but some of it was true. I found that I didn't have much say when it came to some things but was kind of told "this is how it has to be right now" and I was not ok with that. I felt like I was losing control of my life, my identity, and all that I had hoped and dreamed would come after having Ava. I repeated to myself daily "this is not the life I signed up for." This is where it all began to hit me hard. I was feeling so alone in this life of mine that I began to sink deep into a dark place without even realizing it. It's funny you know, because I had no clue how deep I had gone until I couldn't see any promise at the end of the day. Sure, I loved Ava, but felt like I lost Nicole, and Ernest and all we promised to be to one another. A lot of this is hard to write about, and talk about to this day, and none of this is meant to be a knock on anyone, especially my husband, but these feelings became so real and swallowed me fiercely.

For the next two months I put my "got it together face" on while at work and anywhere but the house, but I was falling apart inside, and suffering in silence with depression. I refused to face it, and as I said, I know better, but I could not bring myself to tell anyone what I was feeling for fear of being judged. It all sounds so crazy to me now, but that was the place I was in. I must have been doing a good job because no one close to me asked if I was ok, or if things were bothering me. I cried every single morning in the shower, and some days negotiated with myself that if my husband asked if I had been crying, I would tell him everything. He never did, and to no fault of his own; like I said, I was wearing that "put together face" all too well. Each day I would send pictures to my sister and my mom who reached out to me daily, and honestly kept me going without even knowing it.

All your relationships change after having a baby, and it is so difficult to maintain anything additional that some of them actually just begin to fade away, and that contributed to me being depressed. I was starting to isolate myself, and not intentionally. I couldn't do much having to pick Ava up every day from daycare. There were no more happy hours, or quick dinner get together with friends or my brother in the city. It was just me and Ava until the boys got home at night, and let me tell you, that shit begins to eat away at you. It was during this time that I felt like nothing other than a food source to my daughter, and still being a wife and taking care of my home.

One promising thing came after a meltdown to my husband; he agreed to a cleaning lady, and let me tell you, that did wonders for me to have a clean home. It felt good to have someone else put the work in and be able to relax in a clean home without sacrificing our time to get it that way. My family visited a few times during these two months, and each time they came I said hi, smiled, and shared a little about the ups and downs, but could never bring myself to tell my mom what was really going on for me. I know she saw some of it, but she didn't see the extent, no one did. This was the hardest of times for me because I felt like I didn't have control over any aspect of my life, and not working out really started to weigh on me. I had stopped losing the "baby weight" and was still wearing maternity clothes because I had 25 more lbs. to lose. Sweatpants became my best friend, and who could leave the house wearing those? Even more reason to stay inside all the time and choose to do nothing. This behavior and mind set had continued for around 2 months when things started to come to a severe boil. I was still pumping three times a day, nursing when I was home, and eating like a 14-year-old boy training for football.

Ava being in daycare also meant the occasional cold or cough, and one time it got bad and took the whole house out with it. Shortly after that there were a few discussions between me and my husband where it felt to me like he blamed me for her getting sick. Now, I hate to be hot, and it was June at this point in time, so it was getting warm. I had Ava in a onesie and some pants with the air conditioning on and he did not think that was a good idea. He reminded me several times that the doctor said she needs one extra layer than we do, and that to keep her from getting sick so much we need to follow that.

Now, what I heard was "you put our daughter at risk for illness every time you dress her this way, and it's your fault she has been sick this whole time." Guys, I know you won't get it, but ladies, I know you understand this way of thinking. I was crushed, and at that moment, nursing Ava and all, I let it out...all of it. I cried and yelled and told him I had been depressed. I will never forget the look on his face at that moment. It was a cross between being destroyed and sad, and it broke me even more. He asked me how long this had been going on, and I thought about lying, but knew there was no point. "Two months" I managed to get out in between sobs. He looked devastated. He sat down next to me, and we talked for a while about what I needed, support, friends, family, etc.

I won't go into much detail here, but this very moment re-defined our relationship. What do you do when you realize your partner has been suffering and you haven't noticed it? I think it was a moment of clarity for him too, realizing that he needed to be present more often than he was to take care of his wife.

I started to see a change around this time, and my husband and stepson were making concerted efforts to get home from work at a decent time and help me out around the house more. They stepped up and helped with some things I had asked for such as laundry and cooking needs. I realized I could not do this all alone, and I had been for a long time. Remember, I inherited another child full time at this point, and was bearing the burden of increased chores and meals, all while still trying to keep my head above water. My husband was doing a lot for us, but I needed more from him. I'm not sure how he really felt after hearing what I was feeling, but I know that a change started to occur, and I made a promise to myself I would not keep any more secrets from him. One positive in all of this was that I too got sick during this time, which hit my milk supply hard. Sure, that is not a great thing, but I had been contemplating reducing pumping sessions, and starting to wean off the nursing, and this right here made the decision for me.

I took Ava out of town with me, and while I was away, I wasn't pumping much. I started to nurse her in the morning, and then in the evening and supplement during the day with formula. The week Ava was turning 6 months old the pumping stopped completely and I was only nursing her in the morning, and after work and somehow, I was ok with this decision. I struggled some internally about it, but I promised myself I would get her to 6 months and then re-evaluate where I was. I was speaking with a male co-worker who has a 10-month-old and he said how happy is wife was once she stopped, and we shared a laugh. I told him I was at peace with it, and I did the best I could. He told me "Nicole, you did great and saved a lot of money. Also, you sacrificed a ton of time. Think about the hours each day you spent either nursing or pumping and remember how awesome it was you were able to provide for your daughter". I wanted to hug him, but seeing it wasn't appropriate I high fived him and told him I needed that. Sometimes God puts people right where you need them even if you don't realize.

Getting Well

Sometimes the hardest thing to do is acknowledge that you don't know what to do. I knew that I was not doing well, and needed to get myself into a better mental but I did not know how to do this. I had talked to a few friends about seeing a therapist, but the sound of it sounded so "dark". I am a mental health professional, so it was humbling to be on the other side of "services". Sure, I know exactly what I needed and how I should do it but putting the wheels into motion...now that was a different story. One thing I had told people in my career was playing in my head every day. "If you could feel better, than why wouldn't you allow yourself to do that?"

It basically meant, go to therapy Nicole, and stop

trying to fight this battle alone. I didn't ask for

any professional references regarding finding a

therapist because that would mean I had to tell

people I was in therapy, and who does that?

Amazing how the brain works sometimes isn't it?

I did some online research and found someone

close by, in network, and that specialized in PPD

and women's issues. She sounded like just the

person I needed to start talking to.

I knew what to expect in my sessions

because I am fully aware of the therapeutic

process. What I didn't expect was how fucking

drained I would be after these sessions. I literally

left her office feeling like a shell of myself, and as

if I had just attended a funeral and could not

compose myself. I remember the first few weeks

I met with her wondering when, and if this would ever get better. I had A LOT of shit bottled up inside of me, and some of it stemmed from very old wounds that were never treated or closed to say the least. I also found that I was creating a lot of unhappiness myself, and that was frustrating. I couldn't help but think that everyone was against me and not willing to see how pissed I was about being forced to accept things the way they were. I won't go into much here because it is too personal and opens a lot, but just know that therapy was hard as shit. So, if you ever come across someone who is in therapy, please don't judge them or call them weak. It was one of the most challenging experiences of my life to be in there with a stranger talking about shit that made me uncomfortable. It also had me taking a hard look at my marriage, career, and family and making distinctions between what I had, and what I wanted, which also involved what I needed to do to make sure I was ok. I realized through a few sessions that I was not happy with my current situation and the thoughts I was having as far as how to create my happiness were not as outrageous as I had thought. I had a daughter now, and I needed to do what was best for me to make sure she was ok at all times.

I did fairly well in a short amount of time so my therapy sessions were cut back pretty significantly and I found that it was a good thing to just be going once a month. I also realized that the less I talked about the sensitive things that were upsetting me, the more I focused on what I loved and what I could control. Sometimes I find myself thinking "I didn't sign up for this life" but I have come to the realization that this is the life

God has intended for me, so it is better to accept it and find my purpose than constantly fight it and stay unhappy. Therapy was a good decision for me, and while it didn't fix my problems, it gave me resources on how to attack these problems and address those individuals who were affecting me in an effective, solution focused way. I also realized during this time that therapy done the best it could for me, and I needed to put some other strategies in place to get myself back to a higher functioning status.

There were specifics that I was not happy about but didn't have much control over so I needed to learn how to accept that I had to deal with it, and what was the easiest way for me to accept that this was the way it was. Therapy taught me a lot about myself, my strength and that beyond anything else I was a fighter, even in the moments I felt weak I was fighting. I was fighting for a better me, I was fighting for my daughter, and I was fighting for my marriage to return to some level of normalcy. I had never given up before and I was determined to keep going this time too.

Finding Balance

With pumping in the rearview mirror, I was starting to feel like I had regained some control over my life, or at least my life at work. I was no longer tied to the pump and could actually go for a walk when I had free time or grab lunch with a co-worker without saying "I need to pump first". It was kind of relieving, and I really didn't feel too guilty about not pumping anymore. As a mom you will always get advice whether solicited or not, and it will not always be about things you agree with. A lot of women made comments about not giving it enough time, and the benefits of breastfeeding. Others commended me for how long I had done it. My mom told me once "I admire you Cole, I don't know how you worked full time, took care of home, and pumped." Now, anyone who knows my mom knows how much I admire her, so the fact she gave me that compliment just took me up about 12 notches. She had shared with me a few months how proud she had been of my strength, and that it will be needed over the next 40 years of my life, but none the less, she was glad her mother passed it down to all of us girls.

Regaining control also meant finding balance to me, and this was important in the realm of fitness. Prior to getting pregnant I was a part time fitness coach who ran fitness challenge groups and coached other women on how to get in

shape and appreciate themselves. This was one
part of my identity that I had lost after giving
birth, and I was ok with it because it was one area
I could lose. I realized that now, I needed that
part back to fully adjust to my life. I was 6
months PP and needed to start working out and
focusing on my health. I wanted to be around for
a long time, and I wanted to be able to get off the
ground without the help of my husband or the
coffee table.

I experienced some chronic pain that I
attributed to not working out, and the excess
weight that I was still carrying. I would get out of
bed in the middle of the night and literally shuffle
to the bathroom. It was as if my knees, hips,
ankles all had arthritis and I remember thinking
"great, this is my new normal." I started to
google chronic pain after baby, and post-partum

joint pain, until one day I was like "enough" get your ass back to working out and eating healthy and this shit will disappear (I was hoping half of my ass would too). I reached out to my good old workout gals and leaned on them for support. My best gal in that group was super pumped to hear I was making a comeback, that her comments alone motivated me that much more to get back into the swing of things.

I set up one of my challenge groups that I had run prior to becoming pregnant, and for a while when I was pregnant, and was all set to get things up and running in a few weeks. I made a promise to myself during this time that no matter how hard things got, I would stick with it as best as I could. I would be kind to myself and not talk negatively either. I had a journey ahead of me, but the mere start to this journey would bring me joy and happiness in a way no one else could. My husband and daughter are the lights of my life, but I needed to make me happy in this area.

A couple of friends and co-workers had reached out to be about working out and wanting to get focused, so that motivated me even more. What I realized was that I couldn't just keep eating pizza and fries like I was still pregnant, but I was excited to trade in the fats (all around) for something healthier and more sustainable. Talking with others about their fears, and goals, and what they wanted from this group made me think that it wasn't just about health and fitness, it was about becoming well all around. I named this group my wellness warriors because that is what we are in fact, WARRIORS. We are women, some of us mothers' and some of us strong independent women. Wellness is internal and external, physical and emotional, and a total mindset, and it seemed that we all needed to shift in this direction.

To assist others in their journey I needed to pour into my own cup as well, and that was pretty tough to do when I felt like I consistently ran on empty. One of my favorite people in the whole world is super trainer Shaun T (Shaun Blokker), and there is NOTHING I don't love about him. He played such a large role in my initial transformation two years ago that I knew if I went back to him in some way, shape or form, I would get exactly what I was looking for.

During my pregnancy he had written a book called T is for Transformation, and I had ordered it with every intention of reading it while on maternity leave. Funny right? I had NO time to read that gem, and it was collecting dust on my nightstand for about 4 months now. Every night before bed I would look at it and think about how bad I wanted to have the time to read this, but couldn't even think about it in the near future. I realized that I had become pretty good at making excuses for why I couldn't do things anymore, and that started to piss me off, and actually motivate me. I can do things, and I need to find the time to do them. I decided that I was going all in with my fitness and emotional transformation, but I was going to have to draw strength from those around me in order to do this.

I reached out to my girl gang, my "soul sisters" and let them know what was going on with me, and that I wanted out of this depression and back in control of my life. My coach was like "perfect, this new program is starting and it is really flexible and something I think you could ease into". I was so in and ready for this I didn't care what program it was, I was going to do it. I decided that for the next 8 weeks I was going to give it my all. Get my ass out of bed early in the am and get moving, but I still needed one extra piece of motivation...and that is where Shaun T came back into my life in a different capacity.

I opened his book the night before my new program was starting and had zero expectations for myself. When I tell you that everything I was thinking, feeling, and judging about myself was something he addressed in those first few chapters, it was like he was speaking directly to me at that moment. You know what that did? It lit a fire inside of me so fast and so furious I couldn't wait to go to bed, get up and push play!!! For the next 8 weeks I committed to my personal and physical transformation with two separate trainers, my soul sisters, and my faith and let me just say, I had all the right people in my corner, and they didn't even know it.

One of the most humbling and scary things I had to do once I got started was to get on the scale and take my "photos" from several different angles. Here comes the body shaming and negative self-talk all over again. I snapped those pictures with the fakest smile on my face and got on that scale barely able to look at the number that was SCARY. I remember getting off the scale and looking at myself in the mirror and starting to cry. Who was I? Would I really be able to do this, again? My eyes immediately go to my belly and my hips, my "problem" areas and I just started to unleash on how bad I looked. I promised myself that I was going to get this all out of my system right now, and the next time I looked at my belly, my scar, and my hips I would say something nicer. Maybe it would take me 8 weeks, but I was going to make the effort to do that. My husband would tease me about how Shaun T could get me to do anything, and quite honestly, he was right. One thing I did learn about myself through this process was that it wasn't about him getting me to do anything, it was about him putting the right words on paper to allow me to recognize how capable I was of making these changes. One thing that forever stuck with me is the person I was that day, overweight, depressed, fatigued...was the strongest person I knew because she decided that day to take back control of her life and make a change. I may be in better physical and mental health space than I was that day 3 months ago, but that version of Nicole is the one who was strong enough to make that change.

I literally gave everything I had during the 8 weeks of this new program and really started to see some physical changes. The best changes I saw were the emotional ones that came with a sense of belonging to my girl group again, and being strong enough to run my own group helping several friends who felt like I did. I don't say this to reflect that Ava doesn't give me purpose because she sure does. I say this because my "coaching thing" gave me a different purpose and made me want to show up each and every day so that I could show others who were struggling that they were capable as well. There definitely were some tough days, but I did not miss a day, and held myself and others accountable. I started to really appreciate this body of mine and all that it endured over this past year.

Possibly the biggest moment that happened for me during this transformation was that I tweeted Shaun T about his book and how impactful it was on my current situation, and he responded asking me what key points I took away from the book. For anyone who knows me knows that I almost died when that happened. Shaun T, the guy who has been living next to my bed, and in my basement gym for 1.5 years tweeted ME!!! He was sincere in his message about really being there for people because that effort proved it to me. I had felt connected to this trainer "virtually" for 2 years, but right now I actually felt like we were connecting together, and it was amazing, and it started me on a path that would result in stopping at nothing to meet him and say thank you…with a big hug.

Little did I know there was an opportunity to do just that in a month. A friend of mine sent me this link about Shaun T asking for people to submit their transformation story on this Facebook page, and he would choose one person to meet after his workout and give them a hug. Are you friggen kidding me? It was as if this contest was developed just for me. I didn't read any of the disclaimers or rules on the process, and uploaded a video of me sans makeup and all to a Facebook page that millions of people could see, all in the name of fitness and wellbeing. I remember telling my mother that I was going to win this contest and get my hug from my favorite guy! Shortly after I entered the contest I went back and read the rules and all about the event

that he was hosting in NOVA SCOTIA. What???
I cannot believe I didn't pay attention to that, and
the fact that I did not have an updated passport
since getting married (I know, I know). I was so
blown at that very moment thinking "what if you
win and can't go?" I put everything in place to
get my passport updated and expedited to get back
just in case I was chosen, but it was such a long
shot I wasn't too worried.

Two weeks after the submission the
University where he was facilitating his workout
posted on their page that ALL 7 people who
entered their contest were personally chosen by
Shaun T to meet him backstage after the event. I
was in a meeting when this was posted, and I had
to excuse myself because I couldn't breathe. It
felt like the first time in a long time that the
universe was aligning for me to do something big.

One problem, that my passport had not come back in time, and I wasn't going to be able to make it. I was so sad, and so bummed out about this missed opportunity, but rather than dwell on it I took it as a learning experience. Shaun T was still speaking to me telling me that if I put the work in things will happen. I tweeted him about being bummed out and hoping I could resume my "winning" one day at an event in the states and he responded saying "We will totally make it happen". It was those words that had given me more hope than anything anyone else had said to me in therapy, in phone check ins, or during workout sessions. I trusted this man on so many levels it could be seen as concerning to some, but what does it really matter? I was doing better, so who cares if it was because of some slight obsession with a super trainer or not. It got me up, motivated, back in the saddle and looking forward to another challenge.

After the 8 weeks of my workout passed, I had to post the dreaded "after" photos and get back on that scale. During this process I had gained about 6lbs, lost some weight, gained some weight, but I noticed that my body looked different. I don't use the scale to define me and my progress, I use my pictures and let me tell you, I was impressed with the transformation I saw happening. I was back baby, and I was going to keep going because it was good for me, for Ava, and for my hubby too! The happier I was, the more balance I had, and the more committed I was to my overall well-being was the cornerstone to my family's disposition. I knew I had it in me to come back better than I was before I had my daughter, and I had a whole new mindset and sense of belonging that I didn't have before. I was a mom!! I created a life with my husband, stored that life inside of me, got her out here in the world and kept her alive for all of this time...I am incredible and there is nothing I can't do.

Around this time, it was announced that Shaun T was testing out a new program called Transform 20 and it would be released in the New Year right around my 1-year post-partum date, so I knew I had some work to do to get ready for this one. I had done a lot of weight training in this last program and made some pretty good leaps in my realm of fitness, but I needed more, and craved that motivation, intensity, and focus, so I went back to what I know best and what worked for me before...Shaun T and T25. No one in my girl gang was surprised by this, especially because of the amount of love I have for this guy. I had the opportunity to do a live workout with him in New Orleans and the standing joke was that if I wasn't pregnant, it would have taken several security guards to pry me off of him. Sure, I sound crazy and obsessed, but most of this is just a fun story to tell.

Rising Through This

As I said earlier, this was not something that was easy to do, and there were days where I wondered if I would be able to live the way I used to and feel as good about myself as I once had. The answer to this is no. I do not feel as good about myself as I once had, but I feel good enough about myself for where I am in my journey. We compare so much in life that we even compare stages of our life to others. Living my best life is about living the life that is designed for me, and where I am in my journey. Life is a journey, and you can make it peaceful, powerful, and impactful and a joy to be in. You also can make it the opposite of everything I just listed above. Life is all what you make it out to be, and you only get one, so it is important that you do it right.

I don't feel "normal" or live life the way I had before, and I am fine with that because I am not the same person who went into this journey. Having my daughter was the most beautiful experience of my life, and of all the things I have done before, this one was by far my biggest accomplishment. I don't mean that simply because it was hard to be pregnant and give birth, I say that because it changed me as a person and forced me to go through something that I would not have otherwise had to do. It forced me to become tougher than I ever had before, and actually put me in a place where I had to choose to fight for the will to exist almost on a daily basis. Who would choose that for themselves? Not many people that I know, that's for sure.

I felt things during this time in my life that I never thought I would feel and had a lot of humbling moments too that I am reminded of every so often. No one can ever tell me I haven't been through shit, because I have, and the best part is that I went through it as well. Writing this book was so important to me because I was tired of this being a quiet subject, or only being discussed by celebrities with a platform. When I shared about my depression so many women messaged me about feeling the exact way and it made me sad that we stay so quiet about it. Stand up, yell from the base of your lungs, and get the attention of those folks around you. I wanted to regain control and I wanted to resume living a life that I wanted to live. I didn't want to live in the clouds, medicated and going through the motions. Just because I became a mom did not mean that I stopped being Nicole. Being Nicole is more important now than it was before because my daughter will start to learn who Nicole is and I want her to be proud of her mommy for not staying quiet, and for helping those around her. Before Ava I had a drive, a passion to do things, but now have a reason, and that is to teach my daughter that no matter how small you are, your impact is huge. I felt hers from the inside of me.

Being a woman is an amazing privilege in this world that comes with a lot of judgment and responsibilities to yourself, your family, your career, and your overall well-being. It is a responsibility that many of us don't know we are accepting until we become a mother, and that was true for me. I never knew the level of sacrifice I could make, and never for a minute did I think about how I would respond if my hormones didn't adjust after having my daughter. This experience was sad for me because it had me look deeply into things that I only ever saw on the surface, but if not for this opportunity I may still be in a space that didn't allow me to be the best me I could be for my daughter.

I am not fully recovered at the moment I am writing this, and I don't think I ever will be, and I am learning to accept that. I am learning to embrace my new role, and love when I hear my family say what an amazing mom I am, and how much I love my daughter. If there is one thing, I never get tired of hearing is "wow, you really love her Nicole" because I do. I will wait for the day that I can sit back, have a beer, and really laugh about this time in my life. Maybe I will have lost those last 20lbs of "Ava", or maybe not. Heck, the way my life tends to go once that happens, we may be on this roller coaster all over again!!! Imagine that! Guess I should start thinking about Part II.

There is something so special about learning to love yourself exactly as you are in the space you are in. We are all designed to adapt to our surroundings so embrace your body and minds strength and ability to adapt rather than berate them. That my friend is real self-loving.

In everything that I have gone through one of the most remarkable thoughts hit me the other day. I always wondered if I would ever be "me" again, or feel like I did before I had Ava, and the answer is no. You will never be the same person again, and that is ok. How could you be? You carried a human life inside of you for 10 months, gave birth to that life, and if your life hasn't changed after that...well then, I am not too sure what to say about that. You are forever changed, and so is everything that is around you. I don't drive the same, I don't think the same, I don't do some of the same stuff I used to, and I'm ok with it now. Instead of looking at this as "losing myself" I had the opportunity to create a new me, and better me, a stronger me, and not many people get that opportunity.

I was always so hung up on this thought of losing myself in this process that I never realized I was evolving as a person the way God intended me to do so that I could take care of Ava, and anything else life threw at me. Things still are not settled down, and I don't anticipate they will ever return to any sort of normal, and I am accepting that at this point in life. New life was created and with that comes change just like it does when we decided to make a change in our own lives. Nothing can be as it was before this life because we wouldn't be able to accept this new life. That may be deep to some people, but honestly it is just on the surface of all the things that I have come to realize. Life is all about change and shaking you up when you feel comfortable. Who really wants to go through life just existing? There is so much to feel and experience, and hey we only get one shot so go for it. This was a very difficult time for me, and I get choked up every time I talk about my PPD because I think about how scared, sad, and lonely I had felt during that time, and realize that I did come through it and that makes me very emotional. There are a lot of women who do not survive the emotional rollercoaster and are forever changed or have actually taken their lives due to this.

We as women are exceptional creatures, and sometimes we are so complex we struggle trying to figure ourselves out. I say this to remind you that most of us have a partner in life, and we need to be kind to them even when we are going through our shit. I have realized throughout this time I was not nice to my husband, and I surely took him for granted at times. I expected him to read my mind and figure me out when I didn't even know what the hell was going on in my own head. I didn't offer him the kindness and forgiveness that he deserved, and I see that now. They are important in this battle too, because as much as I wanted to lay into him at times or felt like he didn't care about me anymore I realize that it wouldn't have been fair, and he cares far more about me than I could have ever imagined.

I used to make deals with my higher power that if I made it through all of this, I would be a better wife, partner, mother, whatever just if I could see the next day and see it in better spirits. The funny thing about those deals is that you really are making them with YOU because the only changes that were really made were from within me. I had to change my mindset and want to be happy and get myself motivated to be a different person than I was. Once I started doing that, I was able to see clearly again, and through that clarity I saw the same man that waited for me at the altar waiting for me again now with the same look. Everything within me had changed, and yet he remained the same loving, caring, patient man that had waited his whole life for me.

People always talk about how life gets easier, or the situation gets easier and honestly, mine never got any easier. I decided to approach things differently and find my happiness. Once I did that, I was able to manage what was going on around me much better. It really is all about your attitude and how you choose to approach everything in your life, and everything that you choose to do. I started a little ritual to remind myself that I am in control of every thought and emotion inside of me, and I need to take just one minute to get it all moving in the right direction.

When something triggered me, and I knew what the response was going to be I would just stay quiet for a second. Most people expect a response from you after dropping some news or information in your lap, and it became a fun experiment for me to not say a word for 30 seconds and give myself a reminder that I am in control. It didn't work every single time because I'm human and who doesn't like a good battle every now and then? On the other hand, I noticed such a dramatic shift in my mood once I started to implement this. I suggest you give it a go next time someone starts to say something that upsets you.

You are in control of your thoughts, which influence your emotions.

The Next Chapter

As a species we are conditioned to always think about what is next, and we typically do that before we have even experienced what we are currently going through. Focusing too far into the future with limited experience in how you handle a situation will do nothing more than promote anxiety, and after having a baby that is the last thing you want to promote anywhere near you. Sometimes the most important thing you can do is just learn to survive your current situation, and without knowing you have entered the next chapter.

I am back at work full time, working out full time and working on loving myself and being a better wife every single day. I took a hit this year, and so did my family, but we are working together every single day to get better, and that is our survival for right now. I am watching my daughter evolve every single day, and she is walking and talking up a storm, and it makes me so proud. One thing that she constantly reminds me is that she is OK, and she is tough as nails. I watch her tackle every obstacle thrown at her with ease. She stands up and falls, walks, and falls over, picks things up and struggles but the one thing she never does…she never gives up! She's almost one and has not thought "boy that walking thing is tough, so I guess I'll crawl". She can identify that there is more than one way to get to a destination and she will figure it out. Guess what? So will her mom. I can't be a supporter of my baby girl being unstoppable if I let this get the better of me. I am her example, just as she is mine.

My husband and I often talk about her growing up and if she will identify as African American or White, and we talk about the pros and cons of each one. Our cultures are very different and things that are acceptable in one are frowned upon in another and I am very open about the pressures in the "white world" to be slim and trim and beautiful where African American culture is often more accepting of a curvy body and it had me think back to my childhood or teenage years when I actually learned about body image and what was expected. I remember being a little girl and hearing my mom say she was "fat" and needed to lose weight.

I was so upset to hear that, and I remember telling her not to lose weight and be skinny like other moms because they feel gross to hug. How funny is that as a child I wanted my mom to stay the way she was because she was in my vision a "MOM". She was curvy, pretty and had an amazing body for me to hug. A body that I could curl up on and cry when I had those hard days, and one that embraced me at all stages of life. That is the body I loved and cherished for so many years and couldn't understand why she would want to change it.

Fast forward 30 years and I am working to change mine…funny huh? I get now that it is more about health, at least for me. I am not going to get abs anytime soon and I'm cool with that because I like wine and pizza, and chocolate A LOT. I want to be healthy and strong so that if I decide to carry another baby, I can do so with ease. I also want my kids to see that being healthy doesn't just mean eating a salad, it's working out for your physical and emotional well-being. There are days when Ava is fussy and I hold her and dance around with her only to realize her body is resting on my "baby gut" you know, the place where I can't lose weight, the place where Ava lived for 10 months. My knee jerk response is to suck it in when I notice it, and when I do, she cries or wakes up because her stability is gone. My baby likes that place because it is a comfort to her, so maybe that is why I can't lose it right now…it's not meant to be lost just yet. If I am still telling this story in 5 years just tell me it's because I am not eating enough fruit, ok?

My point in all of this is stop thinking about what is next, or what you haven't accomplished or setting foolish timetables for yourself. I am a firm believer that there is a reason for everything, and even though we may not know or understand the reason, doesn't make it any less significant. We spend so much time looking at what is next that when we get there we look back and realize we didn't enjoy the past enough. I had an amazing childhood and feel like I experienced everything I really wanted to, and some that I didn't, but I hope that I can afford the same for my babies. I want them to get to that next chapter, look back and say, "We had a great past". If you are struggling with bettering yourself, take a break, cut yourself some slack. You can always be a work in progress, but you don't have to make progress every single day. Be kind to yourself and those who love you above all else, for at the end of the day we are truly all we have.

Each month brings new milestones for my baby, and new challenges for me, but I did find that each month got just a little easier for me to figure things out and make schedule adjustments. Being a working mother is one of the hardest jobs I have ever had. At work I am grinding and focusing on improving myself, and my position, and any downtime I have I am looking at pictures of my baby and missing her like crazy. When I get sad and feel like a bad mom for not finding a job where I could work from home, I remind myself that I want to show Ava that it is possible to accomplish just about anything. You can have it all, you just need to change the way you go about doing things.

I was good at my job, making critical decisions in a finger snap moment, responding to all emails at any time of the day, and being able to supervise people and help them develop professionally. My work ethic was what some would call admirable, and just a tad shy of neurotic at one point. I was available to everyone ALL the time, and I prided myself on that. You can imagine how difficult it was coming back to this after now having one huge priority become my only priority. I did not want to be available to everyone all the time anymore because I wanted all my additional time to be devoted to my baby girl. It took me a while to grasp that concept, and that I was forever changed. I started to think about a career shift and remembered my boss at the time telling me not to leave my current role. The agency knew what I was worth, and what I was capable of, and allowed me to be flexible with my schedule. She said, "never leave your job for at least the first year after you have a baby." Truer words had never been spoken, so I figured I would just rough it out.   One of the best things that happened during this time is a new position was created and it had my name written all over it. The position required management of the internal training program, and the development of an external training program that could generate additional revenue for the company. I was already doing training, helping to develop folks professionally, and was looking for a change in my career path (sign noted). I submitted my cover letter and resume right after the "official" posting came out. I received a response, interview, and was offered the job within two weeks. I was hit with a dichotomous

feeling in that moment because I was so excited to
readjust my schedule, workload and
responsibilities, and I felt sad that I would be
leaving my current position and people I
supervised, I even feared they would be mad.

I met with each of them face to face and
filled them in, and they were nothing shy of happy
for me and understanding. The thing about
people is they know you way better than you
imagine. When you let people into your life, and
allow them the opportunity to learn about you,
they just get you. They all commented "we were
waiting for this" and some understood more than
others due to their own situations. None the less
they were fully supportive, and I couldn't wait to
get started. There were some administrative
hiccups along the way, and I didn't fully

transition into that role as soon as I would have liked, but I was on my way.

This shift in positions allowed me a piece of mind when I was home. I had no guilt that I wasn't responding to people's emails, texts, or phone calls, and was able to give Ava all my attention. Another thing that changed was my sleeping, and Ava's. I was getting a good sleep which allowed me to wake up fairly early and focus on ME. Maybe it was only for 25 minutes a day, but I was prioritizing myself. Sure, I could take care of my workouts when my husband was home in the evening, but there is something so powerful about starting my day off with a good sweat, all while not sacrificing any time with my family. I often laughed with friends and told them from 5-6:30am I was Nicole Burke, and after that I was Nicole Kumi, Ernest's wife, and Ava's mommy. I never "lost" my identity after I got married, but Nicole Burke had a different mindset and different concerns, so anytime out of the day I could channel her to kick some serious ass, then I would do just that.

We made it.

Ava turned one on January 7, 2019, and we had a big party with family that weekend to celebrate our baby, and the fact that we made it an entire year. I remember sitting around with her and our families with such a different mindset and feeling so different about myself and our situation. I felt unstoppable, and that there was nothing we couldn't do. Fast forward 24 hours and we were all down and out with some type of bug that got into the house. My Nana used to say, "who let that bug in?" and in that moment if I had an answer, I would have slapped the person. I had never felt that awful in my life, and to top it off, it was Ava's actual birthday and my husband's, and we were all dealing with vomiting and diarrhea. We ended up in the ER with Ava because she couldn't keep anything down, and once she was settled, we became unhinged at home. It is one thing to be sick and unable to care for yourself, but husband and wife being ill and figuring out how to take care of the baby, well that sucked.

I drew the short straw and remembered laying on the floor in Ava's room with a wet towel on my face praying to God to let this pass. It took me 35 minutes to eat 3 crackers, yep, that's right. I was so afraid to get sick again I ate as slow as humanly possible. I made it 30 minutes without getting sick, then an hour, then two and so on. The next morning, I felt like a shell of myself, and so did my husband but we had to push on. Here is one difference with our jobs, he couldn't call out (well he could, but he was worried about the optics). Me on the other hand, I took Ava to daycare and spent the next 4 days recovering from all of this. It's funny because we had just celebrated "making it" and then the roof came crashing down in the form of illness that spread all throughout the home. My mom had called and offered to come back down and help me out. I told her I would let her know later in the day. She called back 5 hours later to let me

know they had all been hit with the same bug.
OMG!!! I felt terrible because I knew what was to
come for them, so I prepped her as best as I could
and reminded her like she often did to me "this
too shall pass." We made it to a year, and then
suffered tremendously for 4 days, but we did get
through it, and no one got seriously hurt.

My perspective changed a lot in those few
days, because I could not even take care of
myself, but somehow found strength inside of me
somewhere that allowed me to get up and take
care of Ava no matter what. I realized how
incredibly strong I was, and that no matter how
badly this last year tried to break me, I was
unbreakable. It was as if I had fully understood
what was going on. Each thing that comes our

way as new moms is meant to test us and teach us more and more about ourselves. I am connected to my daughter in a way many people can never experience. We shared a BODY, not just a bond. She lived inside of me. I protected her then and always will. I cared for her long before I knew exactly what she needed. It was innate for me to do this, and that is because we are connected in such a deep way.

That was my moment, the moment where I found clarity and just sat back with my mind altered. I remember calling my mom and saying "I get it now. I get what you have been trying to tell me, and the things you were leading me to see. I understand our connection now better than ever." I know she was smiling when she said

"Isn't it incredible Cole? To have that connection?" My mother and I have a deep connection and have shared feelings for one another on some beautiful moments. I never understood how some of my friends weren't close with their moms or didn't respect them. I often felt bad that they didn't have a mom like mine, or a relationship like ours. My mom is "my person" that one person who gets you no matter what, and now I finally realized it. We were special to one another for so many reasons, and she may never fully understand my reasoning, but with each passing day with Ava, I understand hers. Your children are meant to teach you just as you teach them, and I can imagine my mom in her early 30's learning more and more about herself each day with each of us. We all hold a piece of her

heart, none greater than the other, for reasons we

were never meant to know, but I have some

insight now, and it is truly incredible.

As the weather started to change and we

got outside more and more I started to see my

baby become a little girl, and a little person full of

personality a good sense of humor. There are

days I look at her and think "omg she is me" and

others where I shake my head and say, "you're

just like your daddy". In each of those moments I

smile because we created her together. The sass,

the movements, the smiles, the giggles, the

crying, it is all of us. One day at the dinner table

she was advocating so strongly to feed herself that

my husband commented "you're so aggressive

Ava, just like your mommy". I laughed and said, "that will bode well for her in the future". I remember him sitting back and asking "really? Where in a bar fight?" "It worked for me. It will also help her in a board room when she is up against a bully, or in the senate when trying to get a bill passed". We both smiled and busted out laughing, commenting about the playground and daycare. The truth is, I wasn't laughing as hard because I meant every word of that. She is going to be something because she is our daughter, and that aggression is really assertiveness that she has already learned. Our children are sponges and I will spend the rest of my days teaching her sympathy, kindness, assertiveness and how to throw a left hook so that she will be fully prepared for everything life (or someone) throws at her.

I tuck her in at night and remind her how beautiful she is, and what she means to me. I make it a habit to wake her each morning with a huge smile, hug, and lots of kisses. I never want her to question if someone loves her because I will always love and protect her. She is my little person who is growing up so big and independent already. There are moments she hands me a towel, puts clothes in the dryer, grabs her shoes, and puts her coat on all to impress me and help me out. I have been watching her intently lately and really contemplating giving her a sibling. She would make an amazing big sister. It made me realize that I don't think too many moms "want" to do this again but choose to because of their first child and the need/desire to give them someone to go through life with.

As hard as this journey has been for me, I would do it all over in a second to give her what I have had in life with my siblings. Someone to make fun of your parents with. Someone to play with, to laugh with, to tease, to protect, and to hold when things do not go as planned in life. My siblings and I are close to one another, and always have been, and I want that for Ava. I want someone to celebrate her successes with her, plan nights out with, offer a place to stay if things get tough, kick someone's ass for her, if need be, and give a speech that makes her tear up at her wedding. For Ava, there is nothing I won't do. If

God grants me the ability, I will be sure to ride this roller coaster again. The best thing about doing something twice is that you have learned from your first round, know firsthand what to expect, and have lived experience about how to get through it. Knowing what I know now, there is nothing I am not capable of.